Tell Me

Deborah Leipziger

LILY POETRY REVIEW BOOKS

Copyright © 2026 by Deborah Leipziger

All rights reserved. Published in the United States by
Lily Poetry Review Books.

Library of Congress Control Number: 2025947183

Cover design and Layout: Michael McInnis
Cover image from *Art Forms in Nature / Kunst-Formen der Natur* by
Ernst Haeckel, 1899, used with permission.

ISBN: 978-1-957755-66-3

Published by Lily Poetry Review Books
223 Winter Street
Whitman, MA 02382
https://lilypoetryreview.blog/

For my muses: Andy Hoffman, my partner, friend, and editor; and my daughters, Allie Nicole, Jackie Lucia and Natasha Lara. With gratitude to my beloved parents, Fabia and Michael, who shared their stories and for my Nonna Augusta, of blessed memory, who tells me her stories still.

Contents

Love Poem for my Body	3
Tell me, what are you most afraid of?	4
God of Beginnings, God of Endlings	5
Migration Memory	6
The Green Ravine	7
The Nearness of Art	8
Dear Moon	10
Lunar Stories	11
On the Night of the Eclipse	12
To Breathe Full and Free	13
Mujer Angel	14
Eve Creating Eden	15
Self Portrait in Countries	16
Cento for my Daughters	17
Summer of Leaving	19
How to Make Candied Citron	20
Shomer	22
Silver Spice Box	23
Whelk	24
Shell Cities	25

How to Blow Glass	26
Painting the Ukraine	28
Shooting the Sculptures	29
Grief is a Goddess	30
Matriarchy of Marzipan	31
Why I write poetry	33
4711	34
Hunger turns me home	35
Monarchs in the Snow	36
The Forest Painted with Monarchs	37
When I was a morpho butterfly	38
Arboretum in the Rain	39
Honeycomb	40
Map of Amber	41
Love's Window	42
How Miracle is a Verb	43
In Hughenden Manor	44
I am offering these wildflowers to you	46

Tell Me

Acknowledgements

Thank you to the T S Eliot House in Gloucester for residencies at which I wrote several of these poems. Thank you to the Vilna Shul in Boston where I was Poet-in-Residence during 2023 and 2024 as a Community Creative Fellow, sponsored by JArts. The Center for Spirituality Dialogue and Service at Northeastern has become a home, where I was able to review and revise this manuscript as a Writer in Residence. Several of these poems were inspired by art shared in writing workshops at the Museum of Modern Art (MOMA).

Thank you to Eileen Cleary and the phenomenal team at Lily Poetry Review Books. I am so grateful to have a second book published with your extraordinary team with so much love and care. I am grateful to Michael McInnis for a second gorgeous cover.

Thank you to Joy Ladin for the wonderful blurb and for her poems which led me toward wholeness in the pandemic and since. Deep gratitude to the wonderful poet and teacher Adam Sol for his mentorship and for teaching me by example, for his blurb, and for invitations to read my poetry in Toronto. Thank you to Laura Mandel for her love of Judaism and the arts. The arts are a kind of eternal light illuminating the sanctuary. Thank you to Danny Leipziger and Maureen Lewis for the opportunity to write in the Green Mountain Forest in Vermont where several of these poems were born.

Thank you to all of my poetry teachers and mentors, including Marie Howe, Marge Piercy, Ellen Bass, Eileen Cleary, Christine Jones, Carolyn Zaikowski, Padraig O'Tuama, Ilya Kaminsky, Donna Baier Stein, Janice Silverman Rebibo (of blessed memory), Nadia Colburn, and Rachel Kann. Thank you to my poetry community which sustains me, including Andy Hoffman, Alexander Levering Kern, Yeva Johnson, Donna Spruijt-Metz, Lawrence Kessenich, Ruth Chad, Linda Carney-Goodrich, Heather Wishik, Suzanne Mercury, Wayne-Daniel Berard, and Jessica Simon.

I am grateful to my poetry Matriarchs, including Joy Ladin, Jane Hirshfield, H. D., and Emily Dickinson.

The author is grateful to the following publications which have published poems which appear in this book, including:

Literary Magazines
Amethyst Review: "How to blow glass"
The Bombay Literary Magazine: "Eve Creating Eden", and "God of Beginnings, God of Endlings"
Call Me [to Celebrate]: "4711"
Citron Review: "Whelk"
Jewish Arts Collaborative: "Matriarchy of Marzipan" and "Shomer"
Ghazal Page: "Map of Amber"
The Hyacinth Review: "Lunar Stories"
Ibbetson Street: "In Hughenden Manor" and "How to make candied citron"
Inkwell: "To Breathe Full and Free"
Lily Poetry Review: "On the night of the eclipse"
MER: "Dear Moon"
Molecule: *A Tiny Lit Mag*: "When I was a morpho butterfly"
Muddy River Poetry Review: "Self Portrait in Countries"
Nixes Mates Review: "Mujer Angel"
Pensive: "Cento for my Daughters"
Revista Cardenal: "Honeycomb"
Soul-Lit: "The Nearness of Art"
SPROUT: An Eco-Urban Poetry Journal: "The Green Ravine" and "Tell me, what are you most afraid of?"

Anthologies
Cape Cod to Nova Scotia: Art, Ecology and Poetry of the Gulf of Maine, Storey Press, Forthcoming 2027, "hunger brings me home"
Voices of the Earth, 2023, "The Forest Painted with Monarchs"

Love Poem for my Body

Listen and you will hear my rainforests,
shaking canopy of nesting hummingbirds

The waves of my body
release shells, oval and spiral

If the body is mostly water
then here are my archipelagos, bays and canals

Meu corpo with its apertures
tasting the world

Follow my river veins
to their tributaries and deltas

Trace the map of my body
hemispheres and countries echoing of shell

Some people say that for refugees,
Refugee is their first language.

I say that for children of the stateless
the body is the first language,

and speaks them into being.

Tell me, what are you most afraid of?

Tell me, and I will give you shade.

Yes, I know of the many ways to die.

Heat   Thirst   Flood   Lightning.

Why fear growing old?

I have witnessed your life.

There are so many ways to live.

Remember, you grow rich in many currencies:

Light   Generosity   Energy   Kindness.

Protect me and I will provide cover

Connected as we are by need and nearness.

I will cover the frozen ground with my leaves

And weave my branches of color over your darkness.

Come rest with me.

God of Beginnings, God of Endlings

Somewhere in the forest
by the Ayampe River
perhaps today   the last two
Esmeralda woodstars
court and create offspring

God of Nests protect them

Purple body   ruby throat   emerald feathers
I hear your wingbeats

In Brazil you are *beija flor*
"kissing flowers" to suck nectar
for hovering

A glittering   a bouquet
a shimmer   a tune   a charm
of hummingbirds

God of Hummingbirds watch over them

When the last hummingbird is gone, what will become of the God of Hummingbirds?

Migration Memory

The hatchlings belong in the sea.

Burning sand stretches out, taut like fabric on a loom.

Heat bleaches the day.

The Turtle Mother returned to the ocean.

Across footprints   crabs   driftwood.

The hatchlings must make their own way to the sea.

One by one.

Following the light horizon and white crests of waves.

Each turtle knows the direction to the sea.

The Green Ravine

In the ravaged city
the Green Ravine
cools you
after the heat island.

The dragonflies
intertwine their bodies
in the shape of infinity.

You hear the heat
lift the *cenzontle* birds.

You sense the lizards.

You feel the water lifted into air.

This is where water is born.

The Nearness of Art

She made Adam
marking his shins
and cheekbones
the muscle striations
his rib cage   his hair
she sculpted him

from the mussel shells
of the Atlantic,
ebony cobalt,
she sculpted him

using only nature's gifts –
coral   flowers   bones
the skull of a springbok–
silver,
she sculpted him

for fifteen years she sculpted
Adam, grinding shells –
each day
she became sicker
losing her hearing
memory
balance
and still she sculpted,
building Adam,
from her "memory of joy"

drilling shells laced
with lead and arsenic

poisoned
by her own hands
her own
Adam

Dear Moon

If I could untether your lunar sentence,
your alphabet, what would you say?

When I was little, I thought you were God
watching over my breath, my silver sleep.

Illuminate the tunnels where the captives are hidden.
Do not forget our babies in incubators, struggling to breathe.

Help us to encode your light, your phases
to create a cuneiform of sky, hieroglyph of light.

Guide the warblers, thrushes, and buntings,
all night's migrants, crossing the inky dark.

Teach us the art of transformation
revealing but also protecting.

How will I know if you receive my letter
in light time, woven across the sky?

Lunar Stories

"A century, a year, a single night...contains the entirety of history."
— Jorge Luis Borges

The moon beams her light stories.
Forest of wonder, each star a tree
each planet an ocean.

How the moon grows like a story,
gibbous, skein of silver thread
even moonless the stories are present

in what has been removed
like words erased from a poem
remain and linger
the unsaid unspooling.

On the Night of the Eclipse

we hover with fireflies
over the bay, Chagalling
over forests and meadows
twilight spooning

the air is warm, engulfing us
we float, debonair
my hair waterfalling
in the sky

To Breathe Full and Free

For Firelei Báez

You cut eyes
into the cobalt sky
to make a tent
of twilight

History moves through us
tunnels of coming and going
under quilted skies
forward   backward
in time's continuum

We weave a past
to occupy under oceans
over oceans   under sky

Living the tilting
wells and swelling
stencils of history

Mujer Angel

I cannot see your face
all I see are your arms curved in blessing.
You are blessing the desert.

Your hair rivers down your back,
the land dry as parchment and leather,
full of marvels.

Your head cast down, reverent,
a gathering of strength
which you give to me.

In your right hand, perhaps
a suitcase, small
with belonging.

Eve Creating Eden

Lady Pink splays graffiti at the feet
of the city, conjuring jungles and story
on murals   gritty crevices   subways

A hibiscus city erupts from her spray
paint to raise morning from night's alley,
she elevates & celebrates me

At night she paints the train
writing the future   calling out for the city
its forms and flora

She paints a moving train
wakes up inside the tunnel,
somehow she knows my name and I know hers

She is my twin,
painting the dark persimmon,
awake inside the poem

Lady Pink paints her name
makes the city her own
tagging and naming herself

Inside the cells of the city
of the train she paints, she must depart
to paint the city's tiger lilies

Self Portrait in Countries

Born under the Southern Cross   under dictatorship
Tangled in the purple umbilical cord
I emerged under a mushroom cloud of grief
With a radar for wonder   amidst colors   birds   belief

My heart balloons with the beauty of the world
My pores open   my throat catches
I burst between my boundaries and borders
My body   cut with line breaks   hinges   blades and latches

My countries open and close
Surround me with barricades and blockades
I hear the oceans parting   ice breaking
The leave taking   the vibrations of ice floes

I seek you out   the colors of your bleeding   beating into night
Your longing   your garments of grief   your circles of belonging

Cento for my Daughters

I hope that I have made you brave,
you in the world, responding to me,
the song I made.
A daughter is a poem.

You in the world, responding to me –
a daughter is a psalm,
kind but not too kind.
The song I made.

A daughter is a psalm.
What freeborn thing
can bear to be loved as much as that?
Write something for me.

What freeborn thing
you in the world –
A daughter is a poem.
There is bravery in being a mother.

You in the world, responding to me.
Being a mother means being someone's god, if only briefly.
Kind, but not too kind.
A daughter is a poem.

Being a mother means being someone's god, if only briefly.
And you cannot understand what I have given you,
all I have given you
to prepare you to fight.

And you cannot understand what I gave you.
You in the world, responding to me,
I hope that I have made you brave.

Summer of Leaving

We wander into your garden.
You gather zinnias for me
to celebrate, to mark absence,
in a few weeks, your daughter and mine
will leave home.

Magenta   maize   orange   coral,
the petals chubby fingers
curling   opening   grasping.

You say:
you must cut them back,
so they will grow.

Under a parasol,
you pick white phlox for my bouquet,
dark red-purple gladioli.

Heat makes everything buoyant.
We float on summer.

You cut the top of a milk carton, fill it
with water
for my long journey home.

How to Make Candied Citron

The citron nestles in the palm of my hand,

the skin of the fruit
waiting to be sugared.

On this icy January day, let the yellow
be a balm, a pollination of color,
a circularity between seasons.

Take a moment for wonder.
Did the fruit come from Yemen? or perhaps from Calabria?
Imagine its place on the tree, in the grove, on the hill.

Italians add the candied citron to panettone or pastry,
my Jewish community will serve
it to celebrate the birthday of the trees, *Tu Bishvat*.

Cut the fruit into hemispheres,
scrape out the seeds and pulp.
The citron remains shy and protected

its seeds dug deep in the snow of its body.

Unlike its cousins, the blood orange, kumquat
and clementine, the fruit of the citron is not edible,
except for the outer skin.

Crystalize the rind in a sugar bath,
a honeying.

The fruit will resist, leathery,
reluctant, holding its shape.

Slice into strips after flaming,
submerge the peel in water.

The peel becomes translucent
as the water evaporates into floral steam.

Drain the syrup,
Add three cups of sugar.

Cook briskly,
Notice how everything transforms.

Sugar crystals forming on the edge of the pan,
sweetness coating the pan, your hair, your hands.

Enter into the sweetness.

Molten syrup bubbles like glass,
the sugar rises.

Snow ice edges the pan.

Pour the amber fruit into a bowl,
crystallized like a memory.
Let cool for the good part of the day.

This beautiful bitter   so much sugar.

Shomer

From on high
I guard
the Beloved City.

I guard
your shelter
your dwelling place
your imagined future.

So close to the sky.
No one can see me here.

Silver Spice Box

The spice box is a tower
guarding the city

Tower of oncoming
night, held
by my ancestors,
handed to me

I open the door
to fill your tiny chamber
with whole cloves

the *besamim*
perfume my fingers

Here is the border
between rest
and what follows

The filigree
encircles
the everyday

its silver spire
rests in my palms,
consoles me.

Whelk

Speak to me of enclosures
of the way things nest
and rest

Open the chain, the casing –
in each receptacle,
a multiverse of tiny shells –
white   whole   bone

Tossed by waves,
disperse the tiny
delicate beings
embossed by wind

Garland of shells
release the crystal whelks
membrane   sand   sound
Empty me

What was once home
ovary
scalloped edges   frayed chambers
Envelope of the sea

Empty me

Shell Cities

For the Calusa, a tribe from the Everglades, Florida, USA

We cannot forget what we never knew
pyramids made of lightning whelks, covering tombs

fossil remnants below,
swirl of maclurites, whorl of ammonites.

We do not know
what you called your people.

The Spanish named you Calusa.
Your Kingdom

created islands out of shells.
land out of whelk, terra-forming.

From hundreds of millions of shells
a landscape of water-bound towns.

We walk your shell cities
unaware of the Earth that holds us,

the buried stories that carry us
forward in time.

How to Blow Glass

Reach into the crucible
for a gather of molten glass

to poise on your blow pipe.

Roll the glass on the wooden marver,
keep it in constant motion.

Glass cannot rest.

Select from the 400 possible colors: tangerine   turquoise
cobalt   amethyst

Roll the glass over the color.

Return it to the glory hole,
let it glow like a candy apple.

Know you need another human.

Slowly move the glass onto the punty.
This transfer to another person is tricky.

Trust the passage of the glowing glass.

Strike the glass so that it severs from your blow pipe.
Then into the annealing oven at 960 degrees.

Glass is hard to rescue.

Speak the language of the sun
as you blow words into the gather.

Prayers.

Notice the flames on the inside of the glass.
Cool off the other end of the blow pipe in a barrel of water.

Painting the Ukraine

For Maria Prymachenko (1909 – 1997)

Maria painted sunflowers and owls
on the walls of her tiny house.

Bright fields under sky
blue cobalt   golden grain.

An orange lion invades, the owls
look on menacingly.

After her daughter dies and her husband,
All she can do is paint.

Death dance of paint,
Dream of paint,
Fog of paint.

Shooting the Sculptures

For Niki de Saint Phalle, "The White Goddess"

You shot at the art

loading up the plaster
with artifacts

from your kitchen
beaters   knives   dolls.

Embedded into the plaster
were bags of paint.

All of the art
bleeding paint.

Grief is a Goddess

Even in the dark
notice the arc of her cave,

how her amphora fill
with stalactite drops.

Listen to their rain,
how their falling echoes

in the pools of water,
how they long to brim.

Grief collects in the ancestor's
iridescent vases

All they ask of you is to notice
their droplets on your skin.

Absorb grief's caveats,
her admonitions.

All that she asks is quiet.
Witness.

Matriarchy of Marzipan

For my Nonna, all desserts began
with recreating home in a latticework of marzipan.

She would gather almonds. Gently
encourage them to release their skins,

Slowly, the almonds shed their garments,
their veneer of tree in the sea glass basin of my childhood.

This is the transformation of matter,
the alchemy of Purim, where we cross boundaries.

This is why we are here,
to soften, loosen the hard edges of judgement.

Alchemy of sugar, breaking of eggshells,
daffodil yolk.

I hear her voice telling me to
shape the mounds into small peaks,

*"let the first layer be a base of foamy egg yolk,
frothy, wrapped in almond and sugar"*

Make room for a new country,
altogether strange and beautiful.

Welcome uncertainty.
This is what you brought with you.

This layer will eventually harden.
Go about your life. Sleep   make love   rest.

When you awaken
it will be new – ready for its crown of chocolate.

Why I write poetry

You have brought your Judaism intact,
your family remaining in Italy

will hide their Judaism, grow up in convents.

How much you relinquished.
Here you are Jewish in the open,

ready for the halo of a sugar coating but

perhaps you will remain just as you are
unhidden   uncovered   a thing purely itself

no further colors   nor outer shell.
This is my offering.

Here is the hardening of time,
the softening of history.

My daughters woven into your journey,
nostalgic for the future.

4711

My grandparents fled Germany for Brazil by boat, sold their house to the Nazis and left the town of Beuthen.

My father tells me about working in the family perfume factory in Rio de Janeiro. How he mixed essences, glued labels on bottles, and packed crates. There were no petals or flowers. Essences arrived ready to be mixed, scent of lemon with bergamot in lavender. Alcohol arrived in drums.

Their Brazilian perfume was inspired by cologne 4711 from Koln. The name came from the street number where they made this "miracle water." In the busy season, my Omi would help in the factory, quickening the process by drying caps in the oven. What kind of courage does it take to sell your home and, with two small children, leave your birthplace?

People always need perfume.

Hunger turns me home

My home is my journey

i am from my leaving

and arriving, from my search
for you.

following milkweed, a place
to lay my eggs

to this promontory of hope

of transmission
of wind which tore my wings

i am from my journey

Monarchs in the Snow

wings cluster
until the forest is orange
laden with flight.

snow descends like a curtain. Monarchs crumple, fall.

                                                                                 The beating

of their wings
create heat

elevating fragile
bodies
into the trees.

A levitation.

The Forest Painted with Monarchs

I
You begin in the Oyamel forest
this temple
of sacred fir.
At the origin,
a kaleidoscope of monarchs   nearly
breaking   branches with the weight
of wings

You map the sun
weaving tangerine sunsets
carried on wings

II
The Nahuatl people called you
"papalotzin" because only
monarchs are silent enough
to travel to their Goddess of Joy

III
In search of milkweed
you rest in its floss
laying your eggs
in the coma of its leaves

The Oyamel forest waits
in silence
for the beating
of your sunset wings

When I was a morpho butterfly

I lived in the Mindo cloud forest.
My azure wings
made from crystals of light
take me through the layers
of the understory.

I layered
with thousands
of morphos
creating blue trees.

Arboretum in the Rain

Here I learned the names of trees

Magnolia delavayi

Here my first kiss

Katsura

Here a hawk descended on the hill

Ash

Here I stood sentry as a turtle crossed the road

Grey alder

Here 400 lilacs celebrate Mother's Day

Syringa josikaea

Here I wandered with my flower mask

Rowan

Here, the sheltering

Wisteria

Honeycomb

i fell asleep inside the honeycomb
the bees called to me
humming, thrumming

i fell asleep inside the honeycomb
the hive alive
the singing, the stinging

all night the bees shared
the language
of pollen, the scent
of stamen
the ringing, the brimming

the sun rose inside the honeycomb

i awoke inside the honeycomb
the dripping, the sipping

the stunning, the becoming

Map of Amber

Faces are reflected here
the dark and light of translucent places

Borders bleed over each other,
over forests and ancient cracks

Sap spills down branches
dripping onto the forest

Injured trees, bleed resin
to seal the wounded

hardening and trapping traces
of petals and insects

Leavings of the frozen sea
antenna hair and wood fruit

filaments of flowers
from unknown places

our countries and their colors change
their names protected

Love's Window

She has been gone so long.
your Nonna beckons you   her face in the sun
she points to the flowers   teaches you their names.

How Miracle is a Verb

Here is what I say in the parking lot after the wedding in Sonoma, to a stranger I overheard in the taco line say that she is expecting twins. Congratulations! Once you have twins nothing will scare you. You will surprise yourself. People will say hurtful things. Call me if you have questions.

What I want to say: The two folded together inside me became each other's amulet. Your body can do the seemingly impossible. My twins have made me brave. You are Wonder Woman and Aphrodite. So lonely you might cry from fatigue. You will learn to jettison perfection, to marvel at the knowingness of twins.

How in Dutch, a *tweeling*
a two-ness double bonded
is a universe.

In Hughenden Manor

Home of Prime Minister Benjamin Disraeli

Fig and passion fruit
vines climb the warm garden walls.
Pears redden brick.

August bees hover,
pink roses in the parterre,
Swan topiary.

Greeted by Byron,
gifts from Queen Victoria,
Disraeli's books locked.

Secret map making
to defeat the Nazis,
locating the past.

My questions linger.
How do you make a death mask?
Out of what? Marble?

Buried in the church yard,
where a wedding just held,
hydrangea bouquet.

A summer Sunday
in ivy sun-filled stables
eating scones and cream.

with black currant jam
silver tea pot with Earl Gray
demerara sugar.

Wisteria climbs
over History's manor.

I am offering these wildflowers to you

this superbloom of poppy and lupine

earth made whole,
wind manifest

I offer you these wildflowers and all they contain
Seed   petal   calyx

wildness
color and courage
brevity and expansiveness

meadowness
mountainess

From this you can make the whole world.

NOTES

Love Poem for my Body: Lawrence-Minh Bùi Davis, Co-founder of the Center for Refugee Poetics, was quoted at a presentation sponsored by the Museum of Modern Art's Writing Club about "Refugee" being a first language. Workshop held on November 13, 2023 with Serubiri Moses.

God of Beginnings, God of Endlings: An "endling" is the last of its kind or species.

The Nearness of Art: This poem is based on the Canadian sculptor, Gillian Genser.

Dear Moon: Inspired by Leandro Katz's art, "Lunar Sentence" and "Lunar Alphabet", Museum of Modern Art, Workshop held on November 13, 2023 with Serubiri Moses.

Lunar Stories: Inspired by Leandro Katz's art, "Lunar Sentence" and "Lunar Alphabet", Museum of Modern Art, Workshop held on November 13, 2023 with Serubiri Moses.

To Breathe Full and Free: This title is from the art installation "To breathe full and free: a declaration, a revisioning, a correction" created by Firelei Báez, a Dominican-born artist with Haitian descent and exhibited at the Institute of Contemporary Art Watershed in Boston.

Mujer Angel: This poem is based on a photograph from the Museum of Modern Art, by Graciela Iturbe, titled "Mujer Angel, Desierto de Sonora" (Angel Woman, Sonora Desert)

Eve Creating Eden: Lady Pink is a graffiti artist who painted moving subways in New York City with Basquiat and other artists in the 1980s. She was born in Ambato, Ecuador and moved to Queens as a young girl. "Writing the Future" was the title of an exhibit at the Museum of Fine Arts featuring Basquiat, Lady Pink, and other graffiti artists.

Cento for my Daughters: This cento incorporates lines from the novel *Libertie*, by Kaitlyn Greenidge.

Shomer: The word "shomer" is Hebrew and means to guard, not only in a physical way but also in a spiritual way.

About the Author

Deborah Leipziger is an author, poet, and pioneer in the field of sustainability. Born in Brazil, Ms. Leipziger is the author of several groundbreaking books on sustainability and human rights. Her collection of poems, *Story & Bone*, was published in 2023 by Lily Poetry Review Books. Her work appears in numerous anthologies, including *Tree Lines: 21st Century American Poems* and *The Nature of Our Times*. Her poems have been published in ten countries in such magazines as *Revista Cardenal, Inkwell, The Bombay Literary Magazine*, and *Salamander*. She has had residencies at T S Eliot House and received grants from the Massachusetts Cultural Council, the Brookline Commission for the Arts, Yetzirah, and the Jewish Arts Collaborative. A former Poet-in-Residence at the Vilna Shul, she is a Jews of the Americas Fellow at Brandeis University. Deborah founded the Lexicon of Change which shares the vocabulary we need for social and ecological transformation.

Author photo by Shana Santow.

www.ingramcontent.com/pod-product-compliance
Lightning Source LLC
LaVergne TN
LVHW090039080526
838202LV00046B/3885